SINGER + PIANO/GUITAR

VOCAL SHEET MUSIC

BROADWAY CLASSICS

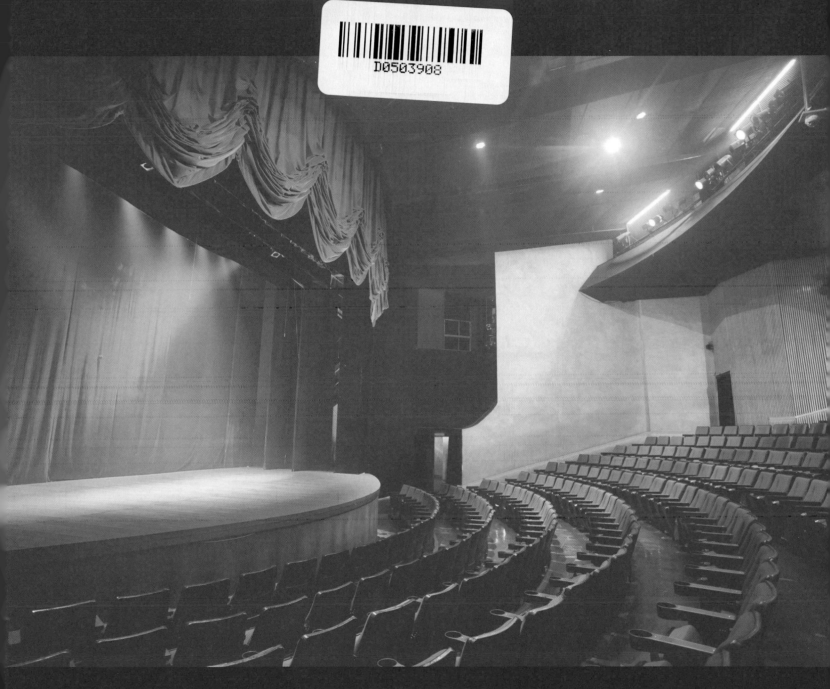

ISBN 978-1-5400-1535-8

HAL•LEONARD®

Visit Hal Leonard Online at
www.halleonard.com

Contact us:
Hal Leonard
7777 West Bluemound Road
Milwaukee, WI 53213
Email: info@halleonard.com

In Europe, contact:
Hal Leonard Europe Limited
42 Wigmore Street
Marylebone, London, W1U 2RN
Email: info@halleonardeurope.com

In Australia, contact:
Hal Leonard Australia Pty. Ltd.
4 Lentara Court
Cheltenham, Victoria, 3192 Australia
Email: info@halleonard.com.au

ALL I NEED IS THE GIRL

from GYPSY

Lyrics by STEPHEN SONDHEIM
Music by JULE STYNE

Moderato

TULSA:

Once my __ clothes were shab- by. Tail- ors __ called me "cab- bie."

So I __ took a vow, _ said, "This bum- 'll be beau Brum- mell."

Now I'm __ smooth and snap- py. Now my __ tail- or's hap- py.

ALMOST LIKE BEING IN LOVE

from BRIGADOON

Words by ALAN JAY LERNER
Music by FREDERICK LOEWE

TOMMY:

May- be the sun gave me the pow'r, for

I could swim Loch Lo- mond and be home in half an hour. May- be the air

gave me the drive, for I'm all a- glow and a- live! What a

Allegro con spirito

day this has been! What a rare mood I'm in! Why, it's

al - most like be - ing in love! _____ There's a

smile on my face for the whole hu - man race! Why, it's

al - most like be - ing in love! _____ All the

mine made the world kind o' fine. It was

Più mosso

al - most like be - ing in love! _____ All the

Tempo I

mu - sic of life seems to be _____

____ like a bell that is ring - ing for

ANTHEM

from CHESS

Words and Music by BENNY ANDERSSON,
TIM RICE and BJÖRN ULVAEUS

Lyrics:

No man, _____ no mad-ness, though their sad pow-er may pre-vail, can pos-sess, con-quer my coun-try's heart, they rise to fail. _____

you won-der will I leave her— but how?

I cross o-ver bor-ders but I'm still ____ there now. ____

BEING ALIVE
from COMPANY

Music and Lyrics by
STEPHEN SONDHEIM

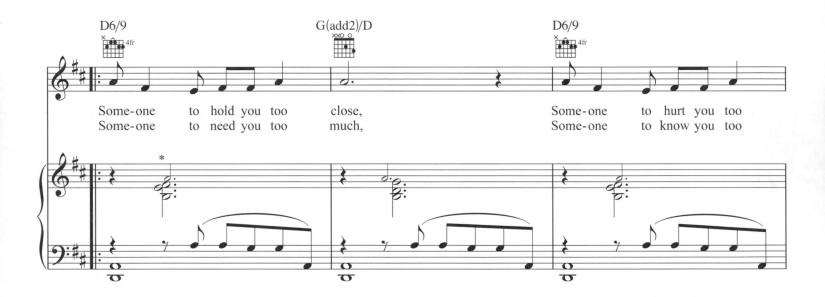

Some-one to hold you too close,
Some-one to need you too much,

Some-one to hurt you too
Some-one to know you too

deep,
well,

Some-one to sit in your chair,
Some-one to pull you up short,

To ru-in your
to put you through

*Add small sized top note 2nd time only. In the original version of the show the first section of the song was in E-flat Major, before moving to E Major for the second section. The keys in this edition come from the "Author's Edition" of the vocal selections of *Company*.

Some-one you have to let in,

Some-one whose feel-ings you spare, Some-one who, like it or

not, Will want you to share A lit-tle a lot, is be-ing a -

*Add small sized top note 2nd time only.

BRING HIM HOME

from LES MISÉRABLES

Music by CLAUDE-MICHEL SCHÖNBERG
Lyrics by HERBERT KRETZMER and ALAIN BOUBLIL

A Bm7/A Amaj7 D/A A Bm7/A
young, he's a - fraid.
mp
Amaj7 D/A C♯ C♯7
4fr
Let him rest, heav - en
F♯m F♯m/E D
blessed. Bring him home,
D/C♯ Bm E7 A
bring him home, bring him home.
rall.
mf

CAMELOT
from CAMELOT

Words by ALAN JAY LERNER
Music by FREDERICK LOEWE

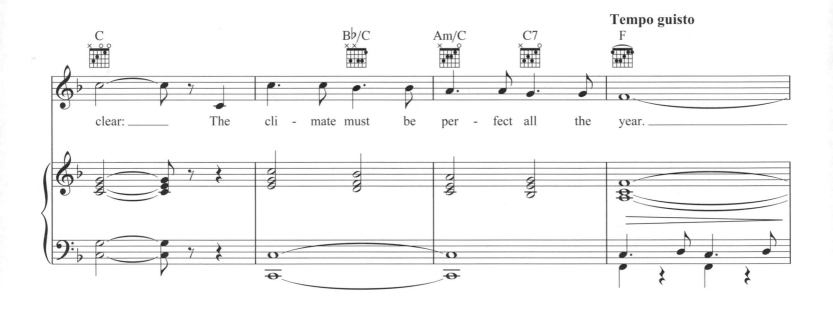

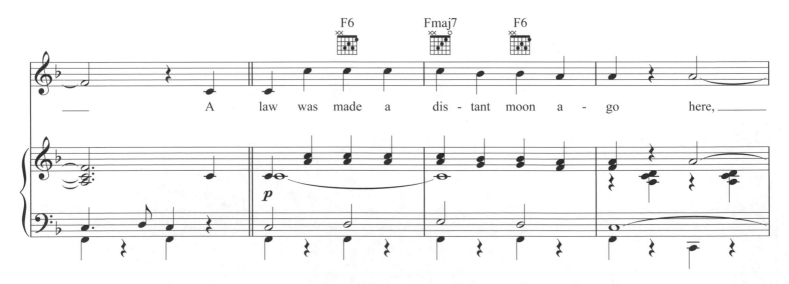

CLOSE EVERY DOOR

from JOSEPH AND THE AMAZING TECHNICOLOR® DREAMCOAT

Music by ANDREW LLOYD WEBBER
Lyrics by TIM RICE

COMEDY TONIGHT
from A FUNNY THING HAPPENED ON THE WAY TO THE FORUM

Music and Lyrics by
STEPHEN SONDHEIM

Some - thing fa - mil - iar, some - thing pe - cul - iar,
Some - thing con - vul - sive, some - thing re - pul - sive,

Some - thing for ev - 'ry - one, a com - e - dy to - night!
Some - thing for ev - 'ry - one, a com - e - dy to - night!

Some - thing ap - peal - ing some - thing ap - pal - ling,
Some - thing es - thet - ic, some - thing fre - net - ic,

This is an ensemble song in the show, adapted here as a solo.

CORNER OF THE SKY

from PIPPIN

Words and Lyrics by
STEPHEN SCHWARTZ

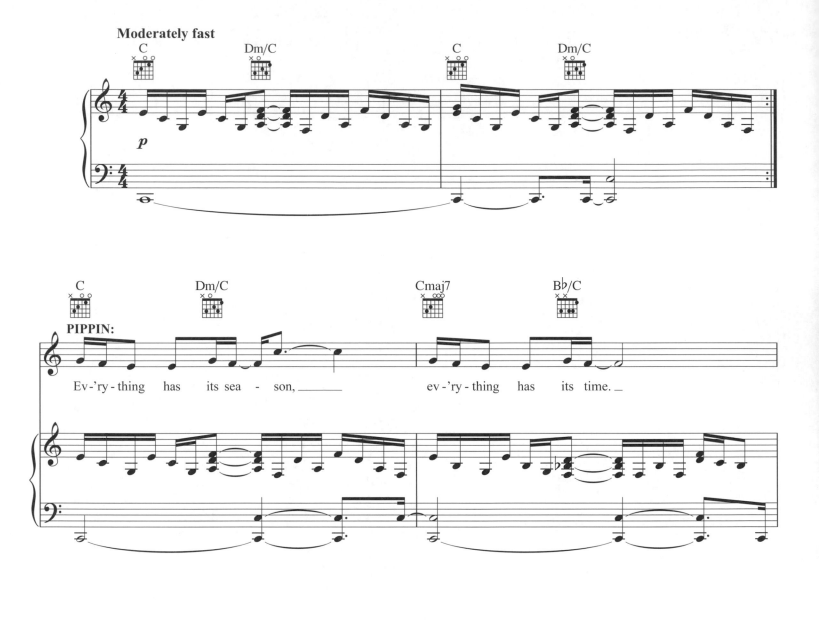

PIPPIN:

Ev-'ry-thing has its sea-son, _____ ev-'ry-thing has its time. _____

Show me a rea-son and _ I'll soon _ show you a _ rhyme. _

of the sky.

DO I LOVE YOU BECAUSE YOU'RE BEAUTIFUL?

from CINDERELLA

Lyrics by OSCAR HAMMERSTEIN II
Music by RICHARD RODGERS

Espressivo

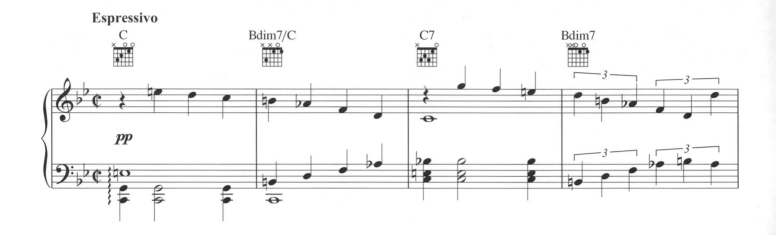

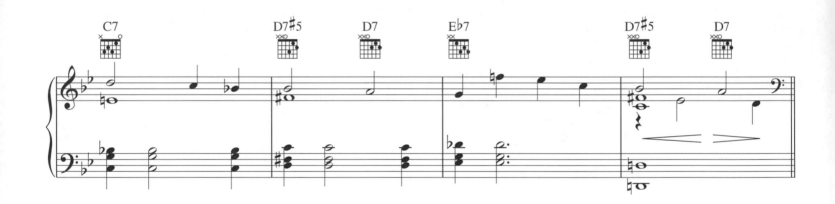

THE PRINCE:

Do I love you be-cause you're beau - ti - ful? _____ Or are you

EDELWEISS
from THE SOUND OF MUSIC

Lyrics by OSCAR HAMMERSTEIN II
Music by RICHARD RODGERS

EMPTY CHAIRS AT EMPTY TABLES

from LES MISÉRABLES

Music by CLAUDE-MICHEL SCHÖNBERG
Lyrics by ALAIN BOUBLIL and HERBERT KRETZMER

Moderato

MARIUS: There's a grief that can't be spo-ken. There's a pain goes on and on. Emp-ty chairs at emp-ty ta-bles, now my friends are dead and gone. Here they talked of rev-o-

lu - tion. _____ Here it was they lit the flame. _____

Here they sang a - bout to - mor - row, and to - mor - row nev - er

came. From the ta - ble in the cor - ner they could

see a world re - born _____ And they rose with voic - es

GONNA BUILD A MOUNTAIN

from the Musical Production STOP THE WORLD—I WANT TO GET OFF

Words and Music by LESLIE BRICUSSE
and ANTHONY NEWLEY

GIANTS IN THE SKY

from INTO THE WOODS

Words and Music by
STEPHEN SONDHEIM

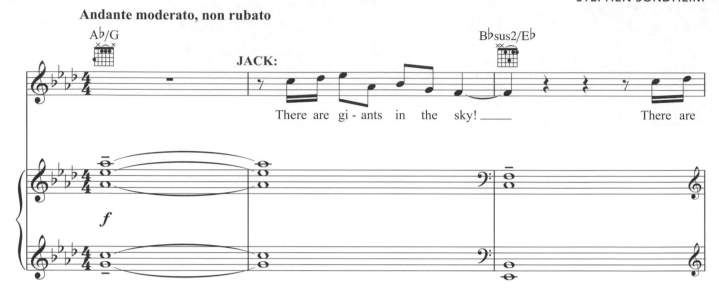

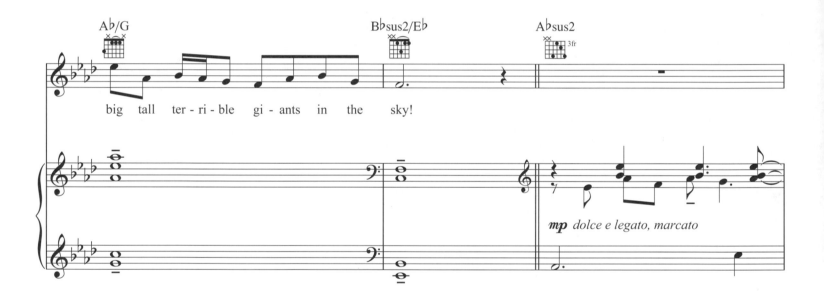

HEY THERE
from THE PAJAMA GAME

Words and Music by RICHARD ADLER
and JERRY ROSS

gliss. black keys

I BELIEVE IN YOU
from HOW TO SUCCEED IN BUSINESS WITHOUT REALLY TRYING

By FRANK LOESSER

FINCH: Now there you are, _____ Yes, there's that face; _____ That face that some - how I trust. _____ It may em - bar - rass you to

hear me say it, But say it I must, say it I

must! You have the cool, clear

eyes of a seek-er of wis-dom and truth;

Yet, there's that up - turned

good, sol - id judg - ment when - ev - er you talk;

Yet, there's the bold, brave

spring of the ti - ger that quick - ens your walk.

Oh, I be - lieve in you, ___

I'VE GROWN ACCUSTOMED TO HER FACE

from MY FAIR LADY

Words by JAY LERNER
Music by FREDERICK LOEWE

HIGGINS: *Marry Freddy! What an infantile idea! What a heartless, wicked, brainless thing to do. But she'll regret it.*
It's doomed before they even take the vow!

I COULD WRITE A BOOK

from PAL JOEY

Words by LORENZ HART
Music by RICHARD RODGERS

I ONLY WANT TO SAY

(Gethsamene)

from JESUS CHRIST SUPERSTAR

Words by TIM RICE
Music by ANDREW LLOYD WEBBER

IF EVER I WOULD LEAVE YOU

from CAMELOT

Words by ALAN JAY LERNER
Music by FREDERICK LOEWE

LANCELOT: *(sings a madrigal to GUENEVERE)*

Tou-jours j'ai eu le mê-me voeux, Sur terre une dé-es-se, au ciel un Dieu. Un hom-me dé-sire pour ê-tre heu-reux Sur terre une dé-es-se, au ciel un Dieu. Years may come; years may go;

Or on a win-try eve-ning when you catch the fi-re's glow?

Andante

If ev-er I would leave you,_____ How could it be in spring-time,_____

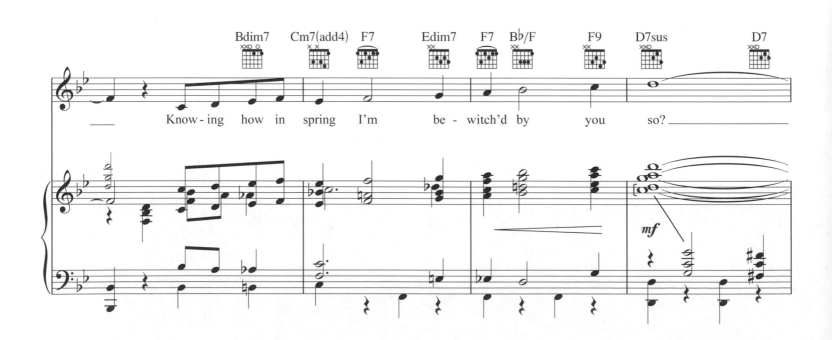

Know-ing how in spring I'm be-witch'd by you so?_____

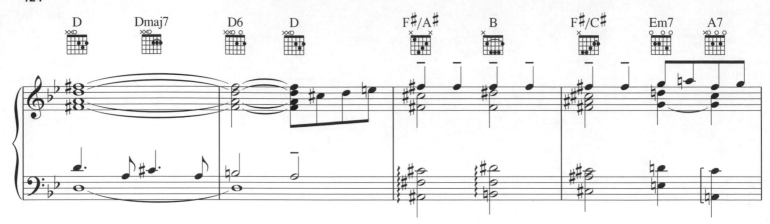

If ev-er I would leave you, _____ How could it be in

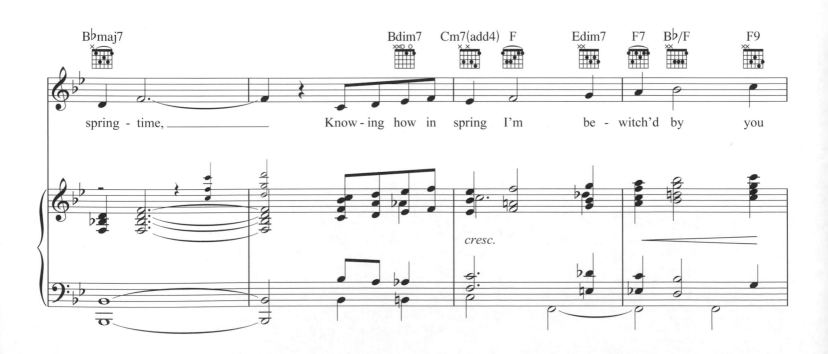

spring-time, _____ Know-ing how in spring I'm be-witch'd by you

The optional notes are an editorial suggestion.

IF I LOVED YOU

from CAROUSEL

Lyrics by OSCAR HAMMERSTEIN II
Music by RICHARD RODGERS

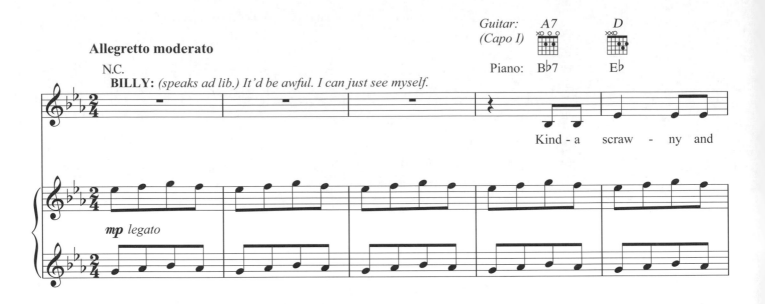

Allegretto moderato

loved you, Words __ would-n't come __ in an eas - y way.

Round in cir - cles I'd go! _____

Long - in' to tell you, but a-

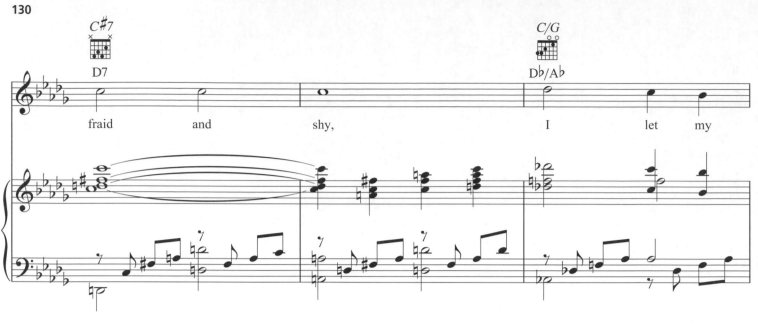

C#7 / D7   C/G / Db/Ab

fraid and shy, I let my

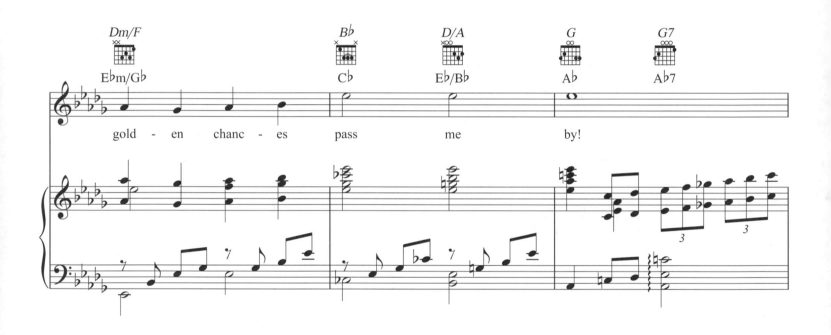

Dm/F / Ebm/Gb   Bb / Cb   D/A / Eb/Bb   G / Ab   G7 / Ab7

gold - en chanc - es pass me by!

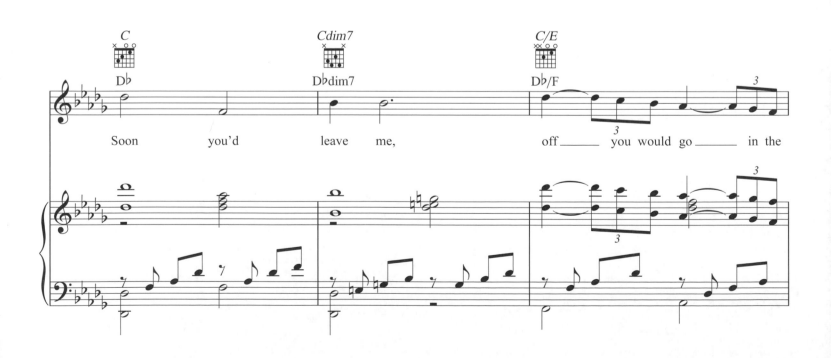

C / Db   Cdim7 / Dbdim7   C/E / Db/F

Soon you'd leave me, off_____ you would go_____ in the

THE IMPOSSIBLE DREAM
(The Quest)
from MAN OF LA MANCHA

Lyric by JOE DARION
Music by MITCH LEIGH

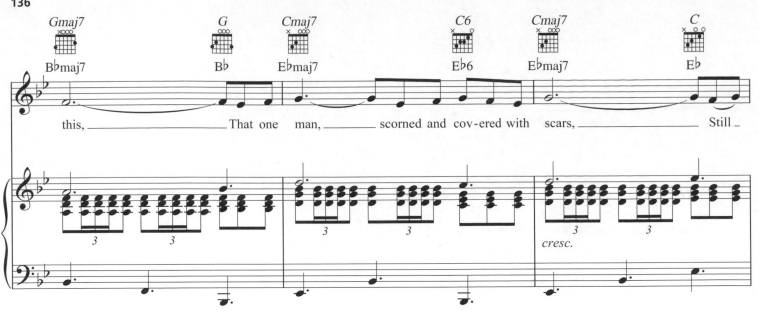

this, _____ That one man, _____ scorned and cov-ered with scars, _____ Still

strove, _____ with his last ounce of cour-age, _____ To reach _____ the un-reach-a-ble

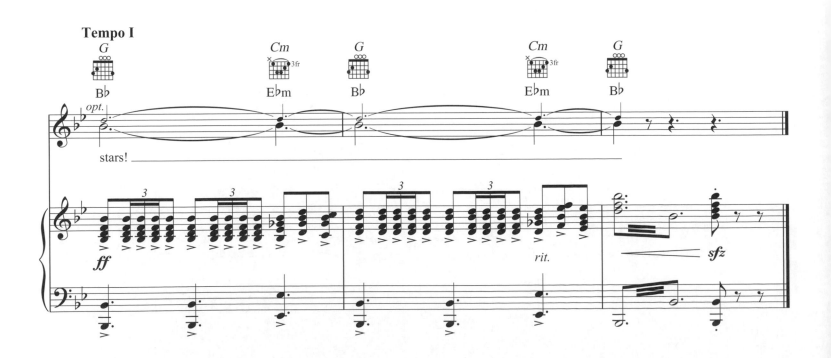

stars! _____

A LOT OF LIVIN' TO DO
from BYE BYE BIRDIE

Lyrics by LEE ADAMS
Music by CHARLES STROUSE

141

JOHANNA
from SWEENEY TODD

Words and Music by
STEPHEN SONDHEIM

LUCK BE A LADY
from GUYS AND DOLLS

By FRANK LOESSER

lush, And yet be-fore this eve-ning is o-ver you might give me the brush. You might for-get your man-ners, You might re-fuse to stay, And so the best that I can do is pray.

Brightly, in 2

Luck, be a la-dy to-night.

MISTER CELLOPHANE
from CHICAGO

Words by FRED EBB
Music by JOHN KANDER

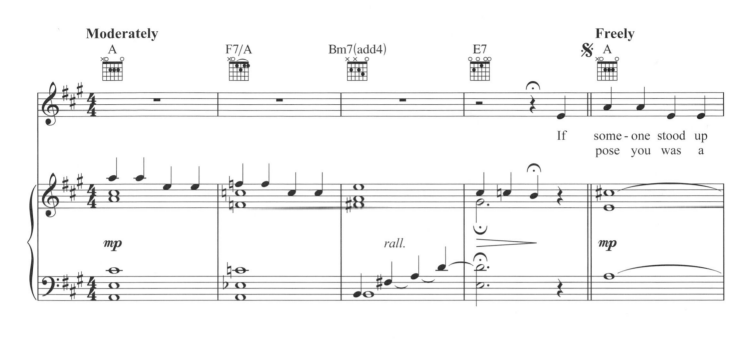

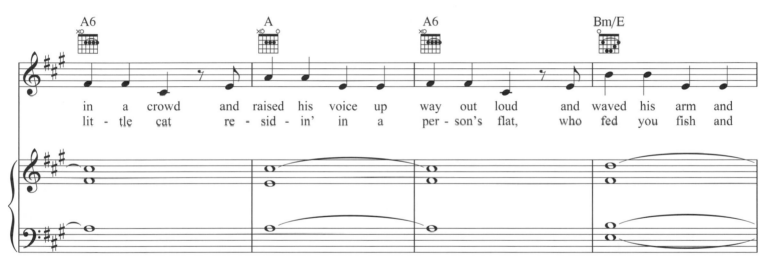

Slow Rag, strict tempo

LULLABY OF BROADWAY

from 42ND STREET

Words by AL DUBIN
Music by HARRY WARREN

JULIAN *(spoken before)*: Allentown? I'm offering you the chance to star in the biggest musical Broadway's seen in twenty years, and you say [you're going to] Allentown?!

Come on a-long and lis-ten to ___ the lull-a-by of Broad-way. The hip-hoo-ray and bal-ly-hoo, ___ the lull-a-by of Broad-way. The rum-ble of a

OH, WHAT A BEAUTIFUL MORNIN'

from OKLAHOMA!

Lyrics by OSCAR HAMMERSTEIN II
Music by RICHARD RODGERS

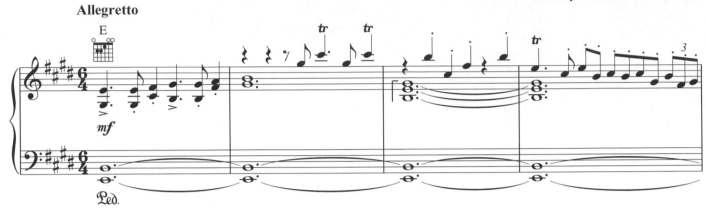

bright, gold-en haze on the mead-ow, _____ There's a bright, gold-en

haze on the mead - ow, _____ The corn is as high as an el - e - phant's

eye, An' it looks like it's climb - in' clear up to the sky.

a tempo *poco rit.*

Moderato

Oh, what a beau - ti - ful morn - in', Oh, what a

beau - ti - ful day. _____ I got a beau - ti - ful feel -

ON THE STREET WHERE YOU LIVE

from MY FAIR LADY

Words by ALAN JAY LERNER
Music by FREDERICK LOEWE

PUT ON A HAPPY FACE

from BYE BYE BIRDIE

Lyric by LEE ADAMS
Music by CHARLES STROUSE

REAL LIVE GIRL
from LITTLE ME

Music by CY COLEMAN
Lyrics by CAROLYN LEIGH

This is an ensemble song in the show, adapted here as a solo.

SOME ENCHANTED EVENING

from SOUTH PACIFIC

Lyrics by OSCAR HAMMERSTEIN II
Music by RICHARD RODGERS

Some en-chant-ed eve-ning _____ You may see a stran-ger, _____

_____ You may see a stran-ger _____ a-cross a

TONIGHT
from WEST SIDE STORY

Lyrics by STEPHEN SONDHEIM
Music by LEONARD BERNSTEIN

The song is a duet for Maria and Tony, adapted here as a solo.

THIS NEARLY WAS MINE

from SOUTH PACIFIC

Lyrics by OSCAR HAMMERSTEIN II
Music by RICHARD RODGERS

One dream in my heart, _____ One

TRY TO REMEMBER
from THE FANTASTICKS

Words by TOM JONES
Music by HARVEY SCHMIDT

mem - ber and if you re - mem - ber, Then fol - low.___

Fol - low _____

Fol - low _____

Deep in De -

A WONDERFUL DAY LIKE TODAY

from THE ROAR OF THE GREASEPAINT—THE SMELL OF THE CROWD

Words and Music by LESLIE BRICUSSE
and ANTHONY NEWLEY

YOUNGER THAN SPRINGTIME

from SOUTH PACIFIC

Lyrics by OSCAR HAMMERSTEIN II
Music by RICHARD RODGERS

arms And fill my heart as now they do...

then... Young-er than Spring - time am I, Gay-er than laugh - ter

am I, An - gel and lov - er, heav - en and earth am I

with you!

MORE OUTSTANDING VOCAL SELECTIONS
from Hal Leonard

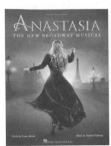

00313505	The Addams Family	$17.99
00130669	Aladdin	$19.99
00241528	Amélie	$17.99
00322334	American Idiot	$24.99
00148752	An American in Paris	$17.99
00172978	American Psycho	$19.99
00197874	Anastasia	$19.99
00322401	Anything Goes (2011 Revival Edition)	$17.99
00313285	Avenue Q	$17.99
00276002	The Band's Visit	$19.99
00250379	Be More Chill	$17.99
00123827	Beautiful: The Carole King Musical	$17.99
00312511	Disney's Beauty & The Beast	$22.99
00125618	Big Fish	$19.99
00313432	Billy Elliot	$17.99
00138578	The Bridges of Madison County	$19.99
00175428	Bright Star	$17.99
00119255	Bring It On	$19.99
00251958	A Bronx Tale	$17.99
00313310	Brooklyn The Musical	$14.95
02502276	Caroline, Or Change	$19.99
00119339	Carrie: The Musical	$16.99
00359465	Cats	$19.99
00322415	Catch Me If You Can	$19.99
00117502	Chaplin	$16.99
00251959	Charlie and the Chocolate Factory: The New Musical	$17.99
00312087	Chicago	$16.99
00119879	Rodgers & Hammerstein's Cinderella on Broadway	$17.99
00156632	The Color Purple	$17.99
00313497	Come Fly Away	$19.99
00250241	Come from Away	$19.99
00313384	Curtains	$19.99
00226474	Dear Evan Hansen	$22.99
02501744	Death Takes a Holiday	$19.99
00313305	Dirty Rotten Scoundrels	$19.99
00313490	Dreamgirls – Broadway Revival	$17.99
00313643	End of the Rainbow	$16.99
00155689	Finding Neverland	$19.99
00123635	First Date	$17.99

00277717	Disney's Frozen	$19.99
00125464	A Gentleman's Guide to Love and Murder	$16.99
00313633	Ghost – The Musical	$17.99
00359902	Godspell – Revised Edition	$16.99
00322252	The Golden Apple	$75.00
00313365	Grey Gardens	$17.99
00155921	Hamilton	$22.99
00313219	Hairspray	$19.99
00322290	High Fidelity	$21.99
00194941	Holiday Inn – The New Irving Berlin Musical	$17.99
00146103	Honeymoon in Vegas	$16.99
00234732	The Hunchback of Notre Dame	$19.99
00313411	In the Heights	$19.99
00153584	It Shoulda Been You	$17.99
00119278	Jekyll & Hyde	$17.99
00313335	Jersey Boys	$17.99
00123602	Jesus Christ Superstar – Revised Edition	$17.99
00251079	John & Jen	$17.99
00124376	A Night with Janis Joplin	$16.99
00360286	Les Misérables – Updated Edition	$19.99
00313466	Legally Blonde	$17.99
00313307	The Light in the Piazza	$19.99
00259008	The Lightning Thief	$17.99
00313402	The Little Mermaid	$19.95
00313390	A Little Princess	$19.99
00313303	Mary Poppins	$17.99
14042140	Matilda – The Musical	$19.99
00313503	Memphis	$17.99
00313481	Merrily We Roll Along	$17.99
00313535	Million Dollar Quartet	$16.99
00121881	Motown: The Musical	$16.99
14048350	Natasha, Pierre & The Great Comet of 1812	$19.99
00322265	Next to Normal	$22.99
00103051	Nice Work If You Can Get It	$16.99
02501411	Nine	$19.99
00313498	9 to 5	$17.99
00122181	Now. Here. This.	$16.99
00313617	The People in the Picture	$16.99
00450151	Peter Pan	$14.99

00360830	The Phantom of the Opera	$19.99
00313376	The Pirate Queen	$17.95
00313591	Priscilla, Queen of the Desert	$16.99
00313525	Rain: A Tribute to the Beatles on Broadway	$19.99
00313069	Rent	$22.99
00313460	Rock of Ages	$19.99
00126814	Rocky	$16.99
14042919	The Rocky Horror Show – 40th Anniversary Book	$19.99
00158983	School of Rock: The Musical	$19.99
00322322	See What I Wanna See	$16.99
00151276	Something Rotten!	$19.99
00313518	The Sound of Music	$22.99
00313302	Monty Python's Spamalot	$19.99
00313644	Spider-Man: Turn Off the Dark	$17.99
00313379	Spring Awakening	$19.99
00322460	The Story of My Life	$24.99
00322245	Striking 12	$16.95
00190369	The Theory of Relativity	$17.99
00313435	13: The Musical	$19.99
00313455	[title of show]	$16.99
00190505	Tuck Everlasting	$17.99
00321950	The 25th Annual Putnam County Spelling Bee	$19.99
00130743	Violet	$16.99
00204751	Waitress	$17.99
00249705	War Paint	$17.99
00450165	West Side Story	$24.99
00313268	Wicked	$19.99
00322260	The Wild Party	$19.95
00313298	The Woman in White	$17.99
00313613	Women on the Verge of a Nervous Breakdown	$17.99
00313404	Young Frankenstein	$22.99

www.halleonard.com

Prices, contents, and availability subject to change without notice.

THE SINGER'S MUSICAL THEATRE ANTHOLOGY

The World's Most Trusted Source for Great Theatre Literature for Singing Actors

Compiled and Edited by Richard Walters

*The songs in this series are vocal essentials from
classic and contemporary shows – ideal for the
auditioning, practicing or performing vocalist.
Each of the eighteen books contains songs chosen
because of their appropriateness to that particular
voice type. All selections are in their authentic
form, excerpted from the original vocal scores.
Each volume features notes about the shows and
songs. There is no duplication between volumes.*

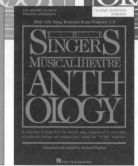

VOLUME 1

SOPRANO
(REVISED EDITION)

00000483 Book/Online Audio $42.99
00361071 Book Only....................$22.99
00740227 2 Accompaniment CDs..$22.99

MEZZO-SOPRANO/BELTER
(REVISED EDITION)

00000484 Book/Online Audio $44.99
00361072 Book Only....................$22.99
00740230 2 Accompaniment CDs..$22.99

TENOR
(REVISED EDITION)

00000485 Book/Online Audio $44.99
00361073 Book Only....................$22.99
00740233 2 Accompaniment CDs..$24.99

BARITONE/BASS
(REVISED EDITION)

00000486 Book/Online Audio $44.99
00361074 Book Only....................$24.99
00740236 2 Accompaniment CDs..$22.99

DUETS

00000487 Book/Online Audio $42.99
00361075 Book Only....................$22.99
00740239 2 Accompaniment CDs..$22.99

VOLUME 2

SOPRANO
(REVISED EDITION)

00000488 Book/Online Audio $44.99
00747066 Book Only....................$22.99
00740228 2 Accompaniment CDs..$24.99

MEZZO-SOPRANO/BELTER
(REVISED EDITION)

00000489 Book/Online Audio $44.99
00747031 Book Only....................$22.99
00740231 2 Accompaniment CDs..$24.99

TENOR

00000490 Book/Online Audio $44.99
00747032 Book Only....................$24.99
00740234 2 Accompaniment CDs..$24.99

BARITONE/BASS

00000491 Book/Online Audio $44.99
00747033 Book Only....................$24.99
00740237 2 Accompaniment CDs..$22.99

DUETS

00000492 Book/Online Audio $44.99
00740331 Book Only....................$24.99
00740240 2 Accompaniment CDs..$24.99

VOLUME 3

SOPRANO

00000493 Book/Online Audio $42.99
00740122 Book Only....................$22.99
00740229 2 Accompaniment CDs..$24.99

MEZZO SOPRANO/BELTER

00000494 Book/Online Audio $44.99
00740123 Book Only....................$22.99
00740232 2 Accompaniment CDs..$24.99

TENOR

00000495 Book/Online Audio $44.99
00740124 Book Only....................$22.99
00740235 2 Accompaniment CDs..$22.99

BARITONE/BASS

00000496 Book/Online Audio $44.99
00740125 Book Only....................$24.99
00740238 2 Accompaniment CDs..$24.99

VOLUME 4

SOPRANO

00000497 Book/Online Audio $42.99
00000393 Book Only....................$22.99
00000397 2 Accompaniment CDs..$24.99

MEZZO SOPRANO/BELTER

00000498 Book/Online Audio $44.99
00000394 Book Only....................$22.99
00000398 2 Accompaniment CDs..$22.99

TENOR

00000499 Book/Online Audio $44.99
00000395 Book Only....................$22.99
00000399 2 Accompaniment CDs..$24.99

BARITONE/BASS

00000799 Book/Online Audio $44.99
00000396 Book Only....................$24.99
00000401 2 Accompaniment CDs..$24.99

VOLUME 5

SOPRANO

00001162 Book/Online Audio $44.99
00001151 Book Only....................$24.99
00001157 2 Accompaniment CDs..$22.99

MEZZO-SOPRANO/BELTER

00001163 Book/Online Audio $42.99
00001152 Book Only....................$24.99
00001158 2 Accompaniment CDs..$24.99

TENOR

00001164 Book/Online Audio $44.99
00001153 Book Only....................$24.99
00001159 2 Accompaniment CDs..$22.99

BARITONE/BASS

00001165 Book/Online Audio $44.99
00001154 Book Only....................$24.99
00001160 2 Accompaniment CDs..$24.99

VOLUME 6

SOPRANO

00145264 Book/Online Audio $42.99
00145258 Book Only....................$22.99
00151246 2 Accompaniment CDs..$22.99

MEZZO-SOPRANO/BELTER

00145265 Book/Online Audio $42.99
00145259 Book Only....................$22.99
00151247 2 Accompaniment CDs..$22.99

TENOR

00145266 Book/Online Audio $42.99
00145260 Book Only....................$22.99
00151248 2 Accompaniment CDs..$22.99

BARITONE/BASS

00145267 Book/Online Audio $42.99
00145261 Book Only....................$24.99
00151249 2 Accompaniment CDs..$22.99

THE SINGER'S MUSICAL THEATRE ANTHOLOGY – "16-BAR" AUDITION

00230039 Soprano Edition $24.99
00230040 Mezzo-Soprano Edition .$24.99

TEEN'S EDITION

SOPRANO

00230047 Book/Online Audio $39.99
00230043 Book Only....................$22.99
00230051 2 Accompaniment CDs..$22.99

MEZZO-SOPRANO/ALTO/BELTER

00230048 Book/Online Audio $42.99
00230044 Book Only....................$21.99
00230052 2 Accompaniment CDs..$22.99

TENOR

00230049 Book/Online Audio $39.99
00230045 Book Only....................$22.99
00230053 2 Accompaniment CDs..$24.99

BARITONE/BASS

00230050 Book/Online Audio $39.99
00230046 Book Only....................$19.99
00230054 2 Accompaniment CDs..$24.99

HAL•LEONARD®

Prices, contents, and availability are subject to change without notice.

Please visit **www.halleonard.com**
for complete contents listings.